Dodo Yeesho in Italy

The magical bag and stick in Python, Perl and PHP Programming languages in the Era of Artificial Intelligence (Level 1-5) with the Italian Barbel Fish, Alpin ibex, Bonelli's eagle, Italian Fritillary and Parot

The Transdisciplinary and Interdisciplinary School

(English and Italian)

Author and Illustrator

Yeeshtdevisingh Hosanee

1

Author's Rights

Acknowledgement

The author extends her gratitude to her family and friends for their unwavering support throughout her writing journey. The author also expresses her appreciation to all the parents, children and readers of this book for their support.

A Special Thought for Readers

Dear Parents, Children and Readers,

This book is crafted to inspire and nurture digital skills in the next generation. Among these skills, programming skills act as a set of stepstones to build Artificial Intelligence (AI) skills in Children. I am delighted to share my creative insights in this book to introduce our future leaders, our young children, to these concepts.

In this book, programming is introduced to children at least 3+ years old. The textual programming language taught in this book is Python. These programming skills will enable children to become creators of technologies, not mere users only. As the children progresses through the book, they will undergo five cognitive levels: level-1, level-2, level-3, level-4 and level-5. Each correspond to a specific textual programming language taught. A textual programming language consists of text characters which needs to be input to a computer or machines. These text characters act as instructions given by humans to machines. The latter will perform the instructions given by humans, creating useful and efficient tasks for us.

I hope this book serves as a pioneering resource in children's literature, enhancing your child's reasoning skills. I encourage parents and teachers to engage in storytelling through this book. The examples provided are intended solely for educational purposes. They may not adhere strictly to real cultural practices. Parents are encouraged to adapt these examples to fit their own traditions and cultures. Thank you for being part of this AI Children community through your purchase.

Regards,

Y.Hosanee

Table of Contents

ANECDOTES

YUPI! I love writing! I will travel to Italy to write my programming codes!

1. Introduction to Computer Programming

Computer Programming is a process where humans will type text on a keyboard to input to an electronic machine. The latter can be in different forms which include laptops, computers or smartphones.

2. Machine and Human Languages

The set of text inputted to a machine act as a set of commands or instructions to the machines. Therefore, humans command machines to perform efficient tasks for them. Machines usually interpret a combination of 0's and 1's only also known as machine languages. For example, one machine can interpret a set of values 00011111 as the word "boy", another set of values 01110011 is interpreted as the word "girl".

However, humans cannot remember the numerous combinations of 0s and 1s. Additionally, remembering each set of 0-1s mapping words is difficult for humans. As it is difficult for humans to remember the complexity of real machine's languages in terms of 0s and 1s combinational values, machines languages are known as low-level.

To allow humans to write commands to machine, high-level languages are used. In our current world, these languages vary from Python, Java or Perl and many more. These languages used English alphabetical lexical to write commands in the form of English grammars, orthography, vocabularies and punctuations. However, once commands are sent to a machine in the Python or Java or Perl languages, machine converts them into 0s and

1s combination to do the mapping and interpret humans' instructions. In order to respond to humans, machines convert their 0s and 1s into human languages or high language like Python or Perl or PHP.

3. Cognitive Benefits of Learning Textual Programming Languages

Learning lexical text characters promote reading and writing skills. The process of programming develops a mental model which creates motivation for children to develop reading and writing skills.

Therefore, reading and wiring skills while practicing programming codes help in building cognitive reasoning skills to think forward and backward in our reasoning skills. Textual programming helps children to auto correct their writing mistakes and correct them in an efficient way, complementing school academic skills. Textual programming develops spatial, temporal, procedural and abstraction skills as children develop to see the big picture of their micro actions.

4. The Set Up

Text characters in programming languages are known as codes or instructions or commands. This book is accompanied with programming codes and children can type these codes on an online editor tool. The three programming languages taught in this book are Python, Perl and PHP.

- ✓ To find an editor for Python Language, connect to a browser on the internet like google chrome and type "python editor online", select any interface you like to use.
- ✓ To find an editor for Perl Language, search "perl editor online"
- ✓ To find an editor for PHP languages, search "php editor online"

5. The book structure (The Story)

The book has five main sections which include five levels 1, 2, 3, 4, and 5. These levels designate the levels of complexity for to learn a particular language or concepts in programming.

Yeesho is dodo bird. As it cannot fly, it has dreams. In a world of magic, the Dodo Yeesho has polymorphous abilities. It can transform itself in different fish or mammals.

In this book, Dodo Yeesho will travel to Italy, a country. While being in Italy, Dodo Yeesho will discover different animals, and he will add his selection on his magic bag. Five animals or fish will be selected through a magic stick. Upon the stick selection, Dodo Yeesho will then turn into these animals and imitate their behaviours.

As Dodo Yeesho will discover their behaviours, he will learn to imitate their behaviours in different programming codes from Python to Perl to PHP. In addition, he will also learn some Italian words as see his programming codes.

As Dodo Yeesho progresses and becomes more acquainted with the animals' behaviours, he will learn so much and become an experts of the Italian zoo. But Dodo Yeesho will also understand their social behaviour and progress through different level. Level 1 to 5. Level 1 being the less difficult programming codes and level 5, the most difficult programming codes to practice.

In Level 1, Yeesho will become the Fish, Italian Barbel Fish to teach Python at the basic conceptual levels of programming in Python. At Level 2, Yeesho will become a beautiful Alpine Ibex, it will want to hop in the Python Language.

Yeesho will go through more advanced concepts of Python in Level 2. At Level 3, Yeesho becomes the Bonelli's Eagle and it wants to protect its children.

At Level 4, Yeesho turned into the Italian Fritillary in the Perl programming language.

At Level 5, Yeesho now wants to be The Italian Parot in PHP language.

The STORY

I am Yeesho and I can teach you Italian and multiple programming languages at the same time.

Level 1: Italian Barbel

Level 3: Bonelli Eagle

Level 2:
Alpin ibex

Level 4:
Italian
Fritillary

Level 5: The Italian Parot

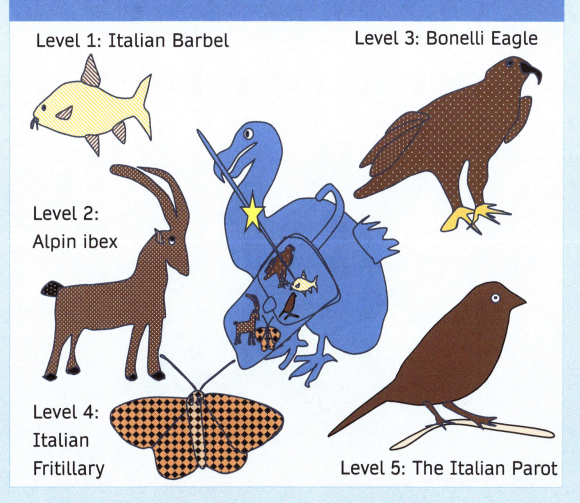

I am Dodo Yeesho. I have a magic bag. I can select an animal with my magic stick. I will turn into an animal which I selected.

Level 1: The Python Language

Watch me! I am now a fish. In Italy, they call me "Italian Barbel" because I am rough as a dough.
As a fish, I will show you my features in Python.

Level 1: The Python Language

print("Coda")

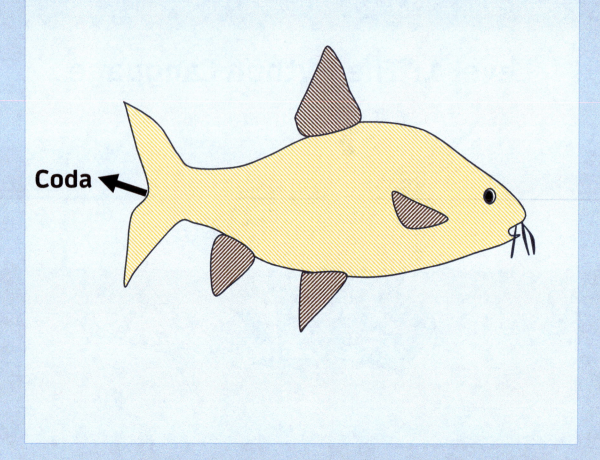

Coda

print("ventre di pesce")

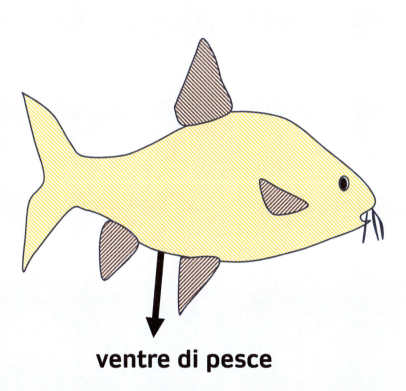

ventre di pesce

print("Dorsale")

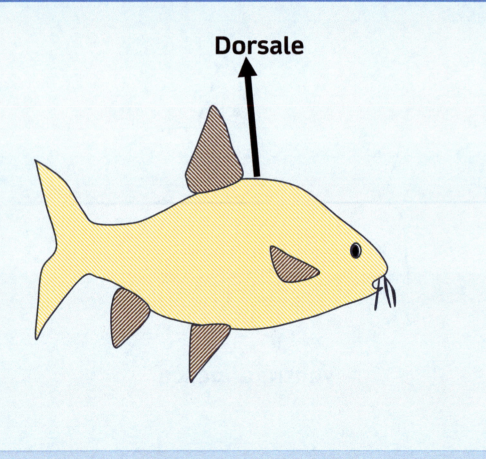

Dorsale

print("Occhio")

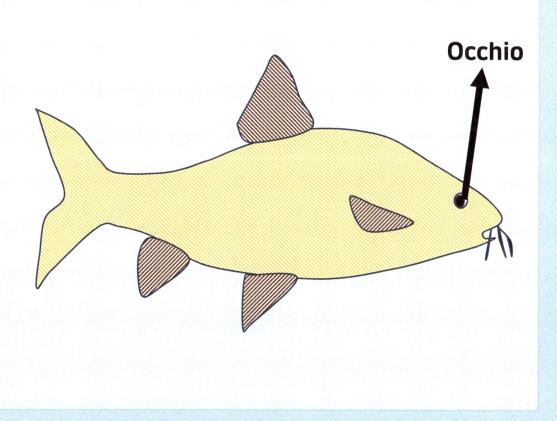

Occhio

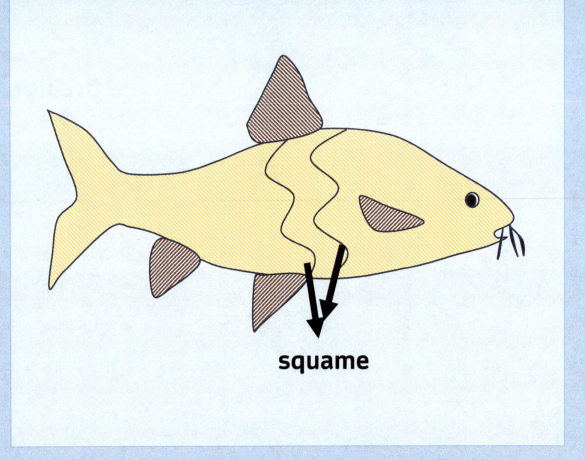

squame

Roccia

21

```
print("Four Barbels")

print("Quattro Barbigli")
```

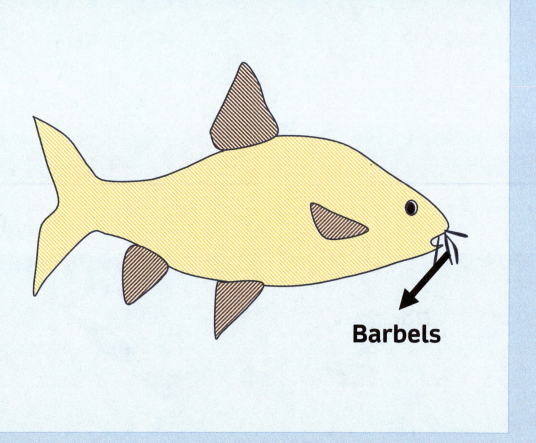

Barbels

22

The Italian Barbel in Python (Level 1)

The END

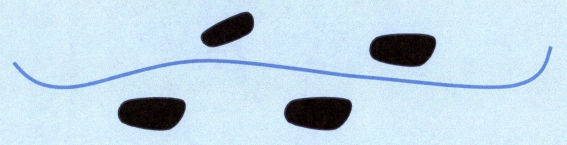

Level 2: The Alpine Ibex in Python

```
print("I live in European Alps.")
print("Vivo nelle Alpi europee.")
```

```
print("I eat plants.")
print("Mangio le piante.")
```

```
print("I climb on the cliffs.")
print("Mi arrampico sulle scogliere.")
```

```
print("The wolves are bad to us.")
print("I lupi sono cattivi con noi.")
```

```
print("The bears are bad to us.")
print("Gli orsi sono cattivi con noi.")
```

```
print("The foxes are bad to us.")
print("Le volpi sono cattive con noi.")
```

```
print("The day is too hot.")
print("We move at night.")
print("But are scared.")
```

```
print("La giornata è
troppo calda.")
print("Ci muoviamo di
notte.")
print("Ma hai
paura.")
```

The Alpine ibex in Python (Level 2)

The END

The Bonelli's eagle in Python (Level 3)

33

English:
The Bonnelli Eagle is eating seeds.
- "eating" is a variable name given to a computer program.
- "eating" variable holds the value "seeds".
- In python, the value are in between double quotes ("").

Italian:
L'Aquila Bonnelli mangia i semi.
- "mangiare" è un nome variabile dato a un programma per computer.
- La variabile "mangiare" contiene il valore "semi".
- In Python, il valore è racchiuso tra virgolette doppie ("").

```
eating="seeds"
print(eating)

mangiare =" semi"
print(mangiare)
```

Eating is an action. Hence in programming, an action can be grouped as a function.
- *The previous codes can be converted into a function to group the action.*
- *def eating(): -> defines the name of the function.*
- *Call the function "eating()".*

Mangiare è un'azione. Quindi nella programmazione un'azione può essere raggruppata come una funzione.
- I codici precedenti possono essere convertiti in una funzione per raggruppare l'azione.
- def eating(): -> definisce il nome della funzione.
- Chiamare la funzione "eating()".

```python
def eating():
        eating="seeds"
        print(eating)
eating()


def mangiare():
        mangiare="semi"
        print(mangiare)
mangiare()
```

38

Every tree distance is 100 meters. The solitaire wants to walk 200 meters distance.
- The concept "loops" can be used to perform this action.
- for count in range(3): -> *indicates the program that 3 repeated actions will take place. "count" is a counter which keeps track of the number of tree to calculate the distance in meters.*
- print(distance, count+1) -> *prints the distance in meters.*

La distanza di ogni albero è di 100 metri. Il solitario vuole camminare per 200 metri.
• Per eseguire questa azione è possibile utilizzare il concetto di "loop".
• for count in range(3): -> indica al programma che verranno eseguite 3 azioni ripetute. "count"

è un contatore che tiene traccia del numero di alberi per calcolare la distanza in metri.
• print(distanza, conteggio+1) -> stampa la distanza in metri.

For count in range(3):
print("Distanza ", count+100)

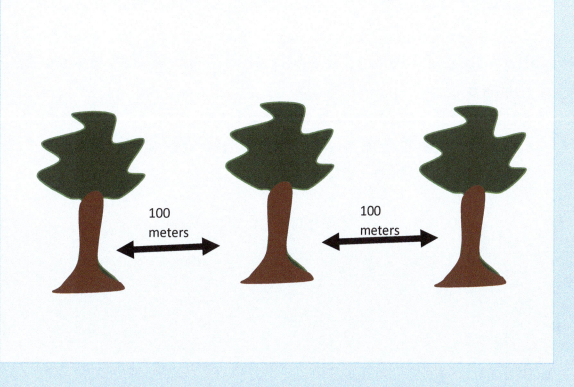

When it is sunny, the Rodrigues Solitaire goes under the tree
- print ("Solitaire is under tree") -> *print the following sentence on the computer screen, "kangaroo is under the tree"*

Quando c'è il sole, il Solitario Rodrigues va sotto l'albero
• print ("Il solitario è sotto l'albero") -> stampa la seguente frase sullo schermo del computer, "il canguro è sotto l'albero"

```
if sun=="yes":
    print ("eagle is under tree")
if sole=="si":
    print ("l'aquila è sotto l'albero")
```

The eagle protects his eggs from predators in their nest.
.

- nest=["egg1","egg2"]-> *add two values in a array "nest"*
- Print each egg values on the computer screen.
- print(eggs[0]) -> *gives value egg1.*
- print(eggs[1]) -> *gives value egg2.*

To note in programming, the space location of an array starts with the value 0.

- **L'aquila protegge le sue uova dai predatori nel nido.**
- **.**
- **• nest=["uovo1","uovo2"]-> aggiunge due valori in un array "nid"**

- • Stampa i valori di ogni uovo sullo schermo del computer.
- • print(uova[0]) -> dà il valore uovo1.
- • print(uova[1]) -> restituisce il valore uovo2.
- Da notare nella programmazione, la posizione nello spazio di un array inizia con il valore 0.

```
nest=["egg1","egg2"]
print(nest[0])
print(nest[1])

nido=["uovo1","uovo2"]
print (nido [0])
print (nido [1])
```

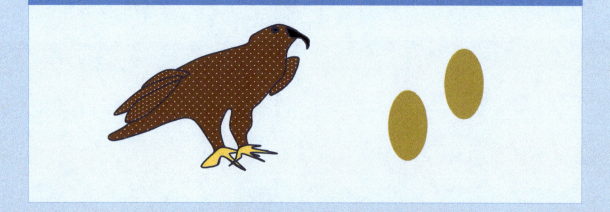

The Bonelli's Eagle in Python (Level 3)

The END

The Italian Fritillary in Perl
(Level 4)

Hello, I am a butterfly.
Ciao, sono una farfalla.

```
print "Hello, I am a butterfly.\n";
print "Ciao, sono una farfalla.";
```

I was an egg.
Then a caterpillar.
Then a butterfly.

```
print "I was an egg";
print "Then a caterpillar";
print "Then a butterfly";


print "Ero un uovo";
print "Allora un bruco";
print "Poi una farfalla";
```

I eat nectars from flowers

Mangio il nettare dei fiori

```
print "I eat nectars from flowers";
print "Mangio il nettare dei fiori";
```

As a group, we like the
sun from Italy.

print " As a group, we like the sun from Italy.";
print " Come gruppo, ci piace il sole
dell'Italia.";

The Italian Fritillary in Perl (Level 4)

The END

The Italian Parot in PHP
(Level 5)

I am the Italian Parot.

```php
<?php
$speaking = " I am the Italian Parot";

echo $speaking;


$parlando = "Io sono il Parot italiano";
echo $parlando;
?>
```

I have a long tail.

```php
<?php
$speaking = " I have a long tail. ";

echo $message;

$parlando = "Ho la coda lunga.";

echo $messaggio;

?>
```

I chirp four times per day.

```php
<?php
$repeat_count = 4;

for ($i = 0; $i < $repeat_count; $i++) {
    echo "I chirp";
}


$conteggio_ripetizioni = 4;
```

```php
for ($i = 0; $i < $conteggio_ripetizioni; $i++) {
    echo "cinguettio";
}

?>
```

I can eat 4 seeds from a box.

```php
<?php
$box = [
    "Seed1',
    "Seed2",
    "Seed3",
    "Seed4"];
echo $ box[0] . "\n";
echo $ box [1] . "\n";
echo $ box [2] . "\n";
echo $ box [3] . "\n";
?>
```

I can eat 4 seeds from a box.

```php
<?php
$box = [
    "Seed1',
    "Seed2",
    "Seed3",
    "Seed4"
];

foreach ($tails as $value) {
    echo $value . "\n";
```

```
}

?>
```

Seed1 and Seed3 are dark colours. Seed2 and Seed4 are light green.

```php
<?php
$SeedNames = ["Seed1", " Seed2", " Seed3", " Seed4"];

$Colors = ["dark", "light", "dark", "light"];

for ($i = 0; $i < count($SeedNames); $i++) {
   if ($Colors [$i] === "dark") {
      echo $ SeedNames [$i] . " is a dark color.\n";
   } else {
      echo $ SeedNames [$i] . " is light green.\n";
```

```
    }
}
?>
```

Bonus with associative array: Show the seed numbers in an associative array

```php
<?php
// Create an array with tail values
$seeds = [
    'seed1' => 'Seed Number 1',
    'seed2' => 'Seed Number 2',
    'seed3' => 'Seed Number 3',
    'seed4' => 'Seed Number 4'
];

// Print each tail value
foreach ($seeds as $key => $value) {
```

```
    echo "$key: $value\n";
}
?>
```

Bonus with associative array: Show the tails numbers and their matching colors.

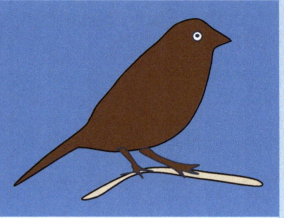

```php
<?php
// Create an indexed array with tail values
$seeds = [
    'seed1' => 'Dark',
    'seed2' => 'Light',
    'seed3' => 'Dark',
    'seed4' => 'Light'
];

// Iterate over the tails and print their descriptions
foreach ($seeds as $key => $value) {
```

```php
    if ($value === "dark") {
        echo "$key is a dark color.\n";
    } else {
        echo "$key is light green.\n";
    }
}
?>
```

The Italian
Parot
in PHP
(Level 5)
The END

The END!

THANK YOU!

The Author's list of publications

Table 1 List of book publications from Yeeshtevisingh Hosanee

	Title	Pub. Date	Age	ISBN
1.	APRAN PROGRAMMING DANS PYTHON (learn programming in Python, English version)	20/11/2021	10+	9789994908653
2.	Learn Python Programming	1/6/2022	10+	9789392274787
3.	Learn Java Programming	1/6/2022	10+	9789392274770
4.	Machine Learning: The 10 Classifiers In Python	17/8/2023	10+	9789392274893
5.	Artificial Intelligence: The 10 Examples In Python	17/8/2023	10+	9789392274558
6.	Artificial Intelligence - The Python Chatbot in Australia	18/3/2024	10+	9781923020566
7.	Diwali Celebration In Python	26/10/2024	8+	9789363555174
8.	Diwali Celebration In Python (French)	2/10/2024	8+	9789363553040
9.	Mother AI For This Christmas	11/11/2024	3+	9798346198673
10.	La mère ia pour ce noël : Les PREMIÈRS CONTES DE NOËL pour les enfants de 3+ ans À L'ÈRE DE L'INTELLIGENCE ARTIFICIELLE (AI)	2/11/ 2024	3+	9782322478620

11.	The Yeehos Tech-Poetry: My computer mimics My Badminton Players & Gardeners	12/11/2024	10+	9782322558339
12.	La fête des lumières en java (diwali): Les contes de Codage avec Crayon et du Papier pour les Enfants de 10+ Ans	2/11/2024	10+	9782322478859